D0371072

Finding Stone

Finding Stone

A Quiet Parable
and
Soul-Work Meditation

by Christin Lore Weber

LuraMedia™

Copyright © 1996 by Christin Lore Weber
International Copyright Secured
Publisher's Catalog Number LM654
Printed and Bound in the United States of America

Cover design by Dan Tollas, Philadelphia, Pennsylvania
Printed on recycled paper

LuraMedia, Inc.
7060 Miramar Road, Suite 104
San Diego, CA 92121

Library of Congress Cataloging-in-Publication Data
Weber, Christin Lore.
Finding stone : a quiet parable and soul-work meditation / by Christin Lore Weber.
        p.   cm.
ISBN 1-880913-20-8
1. Spiritual life. 2. Spiritual life—Meditations. I. Title.
    BL624.W3836   1996   95-45268
    291.4'3—dc20   CIP

Excerpt from "The Dry Salvages" in FOUR QUARTETS,
copyright 1943 by T.S. Eliot and renewed 1971 by Esme Valerie Eliot,
reprinted by permission of Harcourt Brace & Company.

A note regarding the type:
This book is set in "Perpetua,"
a typeface designed by the English artist Eric Gill.
The shapes of the letters are derived
from the techniques of stone-cutting.

APPRECIATION

I thank all who in my life have brought joy or sorrow and shared with me so generously. From these experiences are distilled the stories and the miracles of transformation. I thank the creatures of the earth, the oceans, rivers, mountains, trees, flowers, sun and moon, wind and tide. I thank the stones. I thank the birds and fish, bears and wolves, the deer. I thank my little dog, Ana. They keep me grounded. They show me what is real.

I thank Krista May Kensinger; her innocence inspired this book. I thank Dale Weber, who believed in me and told me so, and sent me flowers when I lost my confidence. I thank Jan Johnson Drantell, who first encouraged me to publish *Finding Stone* and later suggested that I write a meditation to accompany the parable. I thank Martha Courtot, who wrote the little book *Tribes* (Ox Head Press, 1991), which came to me as a gift from my friend P. J. Long. I read Martha's book almost a hundred times, and some of its imagery, imprinted upon my mind and heart, found its way into *Finding Stone*. I thank Lura Jane Geiger, who loved the parable as I did and wanted to publish it. I thank Marcia Broucek for her sensitive, logical, and beautiful editing and design. And always, I thank my loving and wise husband, John, who takes me to the ocean to find stones, who finds me whenever I feel lost, who teaches me to find myself.

To
Krista May
Who continues the story

A Quiet Parable

Once when the world was new,
and the only sound
was the rush of waves against rocks
and the cry of wind over the mountains,
a gleaming, jagged stone was born
from the fire in Earth's heart.

For a million years
she lay in the dark silence deep in a cold sea,
and all she knew
was the gentle rhythm of the waters around her.
There she rested
and learned the sea's wisdom,
which is
Never Ends.

One day a sea creature
hunting for food
scooped up the gleaming, jagged stone
and swallowed it.
She was sleek and silver
with flecks of blue along her back
and over her gills.
She carried the stone
within her body
for seven years.
She swam to the farthest limits of the sea and back,
and the stone was within her.
At last she made her way toward land.

These were the days of trees
that grew tall until they died,
and no one cut them down.
And these were the days of rivers
tumbling down mountains,
shining clearer than the finest glass
through which light passes
unimpeded.

The silver and blue sea creature
swam from the cold blue sea
up the mountain river.
The moon circled three times through its phases
before the creature completed her journey.
She leapt up waterfalls
and through churning rapids,
using all the power of the sea
stored in her heart for seven years.
She swam to a place
where the shallow waters reflected the towering trees
and glittered like a billion jewels in the sun.

She swam to the place
where she had been born,
and there she laid her eggs.
And when she was finished,
she rested.
The beautiful silver and blue creature
lay close to the river's edge,
and the stone lay within her.
Her life was complete, and so she died.

She became part of the river.
Her flesh became food for a mother bear and her cubs.
Her bones settled into the river bed,
enriching the land.
The beautiful silver and blue creature
became part of all creatures
and of the river bed where she had been born.
And she freed the jagged stone
into the tumbling waters of the mountain river.

For a thousand years
the jagged stone tumbled down the river
toward the cold blue sea.
The waters lifted her up,
dropped her into pools
where she whirled for years round and round,
becoming smooth,
becoming smaller as her rough edges dissolved.

Then she lay for a hundred years
where the water was still,
where the sun warmed her in summer,
and where, during the long winters,
ice enclosed her
as if she and the water had become one thing.

At last she was picked up
in the beak of a bird,
who thought she was perhaps a clam,
and dropped back into the current
to continue her journey home to the cold blue sea.

She learned the wisdom of the river,
which was called "Endure."
She learned the wisdom of the sun,
which was called "Receive."
The wisdom of a thousand winters
was called "Wait."
The wisdom of the mountain
with its trees, its bears,
its birds and wild flowers,
was called "Continue."
And the wisdom of the beautiful silver and blue creature,
who brought her to the mountain in the first place
and released her to the river
where she could return to the cold blue sea,
was called "Come Home."

At last one spring,
when the snow on the mountain had been deep
and heavy rains blew in from the sea,
the river flooded to a torrent.
It swept down the mountain;
it tore trees out of the earth;
it picked up rocks as large as bears;
it lifted the stone
from where she was wedged
between two roots of an aspen tree
and whirled her into the torrent.

The river carried her to where it crashed
against the powerful, curling waves
of the cold blue sea
and dropped her on a white beach.
There she lay among other stones,
stones of every color,
stones from the mountain and stones from the sea,
together,
rolling with the tides,
touching one another,
whispering in the language land and sea speak when they meet.

The gleaming stone,
which now was smooth and round,
whispered on the shore of the cold blue sea
for another thousand years.
Often the sea swept her deep into its waters,
but always she returned to the white sands
where the summer sun warmed her
and the winter rains washed her clean.
Coastal winds brushed her with sand,
polishing her,
until she was not only smooth but translucent.
Now, when the sun shone down on her,
she was filled with light.

She learned the wisdom of the wind,
which was called "Flow";
the wisdom of the sand,
called "Change";
the wisdom of the stars,
called "Shine";
and the wisdom of the tides,
called "Remember."

One day after a thousand years,
a girl-child came to the white beach
by the cold blue sea.
She belonged to a tribe called the People.
She had long hair the color of a raven's wing
and eyes like black obsidian.
Her skin was the color of a well-oiled myrtle wood bowl.
The girl-child's name was Shell
because she gathered food from the sea
to nourish her People.

Shell listened to the land talking with the sea.
In their language of whispers,
she thought she could hear her own breath,
the beating of her own heart,
the sound made by her blood as it traveled through her body.
As she walked in the white sand,
she watched gulls riding the wind.
And far out in the cold blue sea,
she noticed a spray of water
caused by her brother the whale.

Shell also watched where her feet walked
for signs of crabs dug into the sand
and places where clams hid.
Suddenly Shell noticed a beautiful stone,
one that seemed to shine
as though the light of the sun lived within it.
She bent to pick it up.
The stone felt more smooth than the softest deerskin,
and it was round as the full moon.
She held it to her forehead
and then to the base of her throat,
and it was warm.

This was the kind of stone her People called
"Finding Stone"
because whatever you needed in order to live,
if you wore this stone,
you would find the needed thing.

Shell closed her hand around the smooth round stone
and thanked the Earth Spirit
who had brought her together with this Finding Stone.
Shell thanked her Finding Stone
for all the years the stone had traveled toward her
and all the hardships the stone had endured
in order to arrive here,
on this white beach
beside this cold blue sea,
on this very day that Shell had come from her village
to find food for her People.

Around her neck, Shell wore a small leather pouch.
Because she was still a girl,
the leather pouch was new
and still empty.
When her grandmother had given it to her
as a gift
for her twelfth winter,
she had called it a medicine pouch.
Grandmother had told Shell
that the pouch must remain empty
until something from the earth
called to Shell
with the voice of healing, wisdom, and power.

*"It may be any of the colors of the rainbow
and must contain the light of the sun,"
Grandmother had said.
It must have come through fire.
It must have spoken with the waves.
It must have listened to the music of the wind.*

Shell opened her leather medicine pouch,
and into it she put the round clear stone.
Then she gathered food.
Before the sun was at its high point in the sky,
her basket was filled with shellfish,
and she was walking through the tall trees
toward the camp of her People.

Shell lived eighty summers and eighty winters after that day,
and always,
day and night,
she wore the medicine pouch that held her Finding Stone.

Shell grew to be beautiful and wise
and honored by her People.
When the People were hungry,
she found food.
When the People were lost,
she found a Way.
When the People became sick from a mysterious disease,
she went to the forest and found an herb
that healed them.

When the People felt lonely or frightened,
when the People cried because their loved ones died,
when the People worried
and when their hearts felt like rocks in their chests,
Shell found stories to soothe their pain.
After many years,
the People gave Shell a new name
to tell her who she had become in their midst.
They called her "Finding Woman."

All this time
the smooth round stone lay in the leather pouch
over Finding Woman's heart.
In the cold
she could feel the stone's warmth.
When she felt confused,
she listened for the stone's voice.
As she lived,
she learned Finding Stone's wisdom.

As she wondered how to grow
from being a girl into being a woman,
she heard the Finding Stone whisper,
"Flow."
As she wondered how to give
the gift that was herself
to the People she loved,
she heard the Finding Stone whisper,
"Shine."
As she wondered how people learned to trust one another,
she heard the Finding Stone whisper,
"Receive."

As she wondered how to pass her wisdom on
to the children born from her body and her soul,
she heard the Finding Stone whisper,
"Change."
As she wondered how to help her own children
find their way along the confusing paths of the world,
she heard her Finding Stone whisper,
"Wait."

As she lost people whom she loved
because they traveled to the prairie
or the mountain or the desert or another sea,
or because they made the final journey to the stars,
she felt empty in her heart,
but she heard her Finding Stone whisper,
"Endure."
As she grew old and was alone,
she heard her Finding Stone whisper,
"Continue."

As the young came to her for wisdom,
she heard her Finding Stone whisper,
"Remember."
And as her body became like a winter leaf
blown across the snow,
she heard her Finding Stone whisper,
"Come Home."

Finding Woman went down to the white beach
by the cold blue sea.
She lifted her medicine pouch from around her neck
and removed the Finding Stone.
She placed it on the beach,
and it caught the light of the setting sun
as it lingered at the edge
between the grey-blue water and the sky.
She listened to the whispered language of land and sea,
talking.
She felt she was complete.

Finding Woman looked for a long time
at the smooth round stone
lying on the sand,
catching the last light of the setting sun.
"Someone will find you," she said.

"Never Ends,"
the Finding Stone whispered back
into her soul.

Soul-Work Meditation

Once when the world was new . . .

I am worlds yet unborn. Each day is new. Each moment. Nothing from the past can hinder me; it does not exist. The only sound is what is now; reality is here. Each moment is the moment of birth. I came through fire, endured unspeakable pain, felt abandoned and alone. It was preparation. Now is the moment of creation. It is the moment to begin.

And the only sound
Was the rush of waves against rocks
And the cry of wind over the mountains.

I can breathe again. Where this morning I was nothing, I am silent now. It is not an empty silence. It is a natural silence. The silence of wind, of waves, of breath, of the beating of my heart. It is a space in my soul for being aware. It is a silence that listens, gently, taking notice. I can simply Be. I am the space within. I am the round sky and the firm earth. The waves of life wash through me, and the wind of spirit cries in my heart.

A gleaming, jagged stone was born
From the fire in Earth's heart.

Opposites merge in me. I am fire and water; I am earth. I come from deep, from the center, from where everything is one. I am molten rock, shining, curling up from fissures in earth's crust, meeting water, steaming, taking form. No wonder I have known conflict. No wonder I have been splintered, broken, uncertain who I am. I am granite; I am diamond. I am dense and clear. I am made of fire from the heart of earth. I am washed by water in the womb of God. I am born. And yet again, I am born.

For a million years
She lay in the dark silence deep in a cold sea.

Waiting is endless. I waited to be grown up, to become myself, to be smart enough, patient enough, wise enough, loving enough. I waited to be seen, to be heard, to be recognized. Even now, I wait to be called by name, to be understood. I wait to be strong. I wait to dare. I wait because I am powerless to do anything else. I wait because what I most treasure is what is deepest within and protected by silence. Out of waiting comes patience. Out of accepting my powerlessness comes strength and love and the courage to dare. I wait and the waters enclose me: the waters of compassion, of Divine Mercy and tenderness. I wait in the womb of God.

And all she knew
Was the gentle rhythm of the waters around her.

I am more than I am. I close my eyes. My whole body pounds, thunders, swells. I am the ocean. My boundaries dissolve. I am the rain. The rhythm of being is subtle. At other times I rush about, distracted by the noise of this or that possibility, haunted by the lure of popularity or status, superficial pleasure or power. I lose my sense of rhythm. I forget to be gentle with myself. I do not feel the flow of life. I lose my connection with that Greater Being. The subtle rhythm of Greater Being teaches how to move, how to know what is vital. Even when I am battered on all sides by the noise of the world, I require only the slightest turn in my awareness to feel the essential rhythm at its core. My own rhythm is the rhythm of the universe. It is within and around me. It reminds me who I am, what I need, and how to live in gentleness.

There she rested
And learned the sea's wisdom,
Which is
Never Ends.

Life is change. But I do not want the day to end, and when it is night, I do not want the moon to set. I want the rocks along the shore of my childhood to stay the same; the quartz rock on which I stood to watch the gulls soar, I do not want it to wear away. I want the woods to stay. I want the path to be free of brambles. I want what gives me joy; I want my mother always alive. I fear endings, so I hold on. I attempt to control. I fail. I make myself tense with failing. Such is not the wisdom of Never Ends. The waters flow, they ebb. What was, is not. What is not, becomes. Death and life flow into and from one another. Nothing stands still. Waves pulled the quartz rock into deep water; where the grove stood tall in the woods, lady-slippers grow.

One day a sea creature
Hunting for food
Scooped up the gleaming, jagged stone
And swallowed it.

Things happen. They cannot be explained. They cannot be anticipated. Things happen that change our lives. Someone I meet, someone in need, turns out to be the one who lifts me up and carries me beyond imagination. Or some forgotten part of myself suddenly takes hold; I am scooped up, held, transported. These things can be terrible, things that consume. I am eaten by life. Illness, death, failure, these things happen. I feel swallowed up. Lost. These things can also be wondrous. I am lifted out of pain, out of loneliness, out of a paralysis of creative energy. I am moved. I know that I am going somewhere. Whether by wonder or by terror, I am taken up. I am not in control. I am at the mercy of the Sea, the Source of all life.

She was sleek and silver
With flecks of blue along her back
And over her gills.

The One who holds my life is Beauty beyond telling. This is hard to believe when all I see is darkness. It is hard to believe when I do not know where I am headed. I have lost things, things I thought essential. Life depended on them! A lover, a child, a home, a job, a dream. I went along from day to day, deliberately surviving, and that was all. I went along picking up one foot and setting it down, over and over. I ate cereal because it was easy. I stared at the television. I forgot how to sing. And then one day, miraculously, when I set that one foot in front of the other, I found myself someplace else. A place of hope. A place of new life. I do not know how I got there. I must have been carried along by a Mercy of which I was not aware. Something must have been taking care of me because I certainly was not taking care of myself. Something sleek and silver brought me through. Something beautiful.

She carried the stone
Within her body
For seven years.

What surrounds me is endless. It is night, and I am not asleep. I lean in against a membrane of breath. I float. I am a stone, a focused point. I am an egg, a seed, in the Eternal Womb. Life is pregnant with me. I am pregnant with myself. God is pregnant with life. I carry the gleaming, jagged essence of being, that paradox of fire and rock, spirit and body. I carry it and do not know I carry it. I carry it as the sea creature carries the stone, unaware. And I am carried by a larger Life. I am a circle within circles of being and the possibility of being. The circles do not end.

She swam to the farthest limits of the sea and back,
And the stone was within her.
At last she made her way toward land.

I cannot measure the limits of my possibilities. Who knows of what I am capable?

"I will be tenacious," my friend whispers as she swims against the currents of her oncoming death, as she touches every shoreline of her life, as she finally allows the full tide of this final experience to carry her, bring her to the place of her beginning. "Will you be tenacious?" she questions me and her eyes burn.

"I will."

She holds me with those eyes. She is not finished with me yet. "Promise!" she demands.

"I promise."

I am learning the extent of that commitment. I touch every shore. I swim the dark expanse. I swim the depths and swim the shallows. I chart my way by the stars, by the sun, by the moon. And when clouds obscure the sky, I feel the currents around and within. I trust them now. They will take me home.

These were the days of trees
That grew tall until they died,
And no one cut them down.

Trees tower in my soul. I am a tree, rooted in earth, arms in the sky, laden with flowers and fruit. I dream of trees connecting the realms of being within me, the ground of my body with the flowers of Divine Life. I must take care over what in myself I decide to cut down. I can grow: I can reach deep into earth; I can touch the sky; I will flower. I can grow until I die.

And these were the days of rivers
Tumbling down mountains,
Shining clearer than the finest glass
Through which light passes
Unimpeded.

Clarity is the work of a lifetime. I will not cloud my spirit. I am a mountain stream. I am water shimmering with light. No longer will I sicken my heart with lies. No longer will I cloud my mind with illusion that keeps light from getting through. Fear and anger suffocate. I let them go; I let them wash away. Settled sludge lifts from my depth: old leaves, lost hopes, every waste and guilt and shame, the dreams that died. I let the current take them. I become clear all the way to the bottom. The river bed reflects the sun. I become again the clear water of innocence.

The silver and blue sea creature
Swam from the cold blue sea
Up the mountain river.

Leaving and returning is a cycle of life. I leave home for a strange place. Everything is different. I am accustomed to plains where the land shimmers into the sky at the horizon and the sky appears endless. Where storm clouds can be seen coming for fifty miles. Where rain is a grey curtain waving in the distance. Here, mountains cut the clouds. Here, rain comes only in winter. I am accustomed to snow and bare tree branches. Here, Christmas is green. Here, I feel the constant pulse of the sea. Here, I am a stranger. I must return home.

I visit a friend. I gaze over the familiar plains and feel a pang of nostalgia. But at this place I call home, I miss the faint smell of sea salt on the wind. I turn again to where the rounded, womanly hills await the winter rains. I leave and I return. I am stranger and friend. But home is within me.

The moon circled three times through its phases
Before the creature completed her journey.

Awareness and memory carry life forward. The closer I am to the fulfillment of something, the more I notice time. I have counted days. I have counted hours. I have counted the breaths of loved ones dying and the moments they represented. I mark time to make myself aware. I notice the details of the times and make them into stories to celebrate my awareness and to remember. I tell the stories to children. I discover what I am from the reflection in their eyes. I identify and create myself. I thank them and move on.

She leapt up waterfalls
And through churning rapids,
Using all the power of the sea
Stored in her heart for seven years.

The way home is within me. I find my way like salmon smelling the waters of the place they were spawned. If there is a trickle of water from the stream of their origin, the salmon find it. They do anything to get there. And I? I am still on the move. Still catching the scent. I can say this: I have seen others find their way. Many of them are older, women and men who seem to lean back into their lives as if they could rest in themselves. They like who they are. They laugh. They do not expect to be everything to everyone. They do not expect to live forever. I learn from them. I use the power stored in my heart to find my way home.

She swam to a place
Where the shallow waters reflected the towering trees
And glittered like a billion jewels in the sun.

I will know the place. It is quiet there. All the voices of shame and condemnation keep silence. No one says, "I expected this of you," or "It's not perfect yet." The deepest whispers cease, the whispers of "You were doomed from the beginning; you never had a chance." If I hear those voices in my mind, I am not yet home. I am not yet face-to-face with my most essential self. I will know the place. I am beautiful there. Breathtaking. It is the place of my beginning; it is the place of my ending; it is the place where I am whole. It is worth the journey. It is worth the hardships, the leaping up waterfalls, the drawing forth of courage I never knew I had. It is worth the absolute darkness, when all I can do is lie silent at the bottom, so deep no light can reach. It is worth the doubts, the questioning—am I going anywhere at all? It is worth, as the poet says, "A lifetime's death in love." I will know the place. It is my true self.

She swam to the place
where she had been born,
And there she laid her eggs.
And when she was finished,
she rested.

I make a circle of my life. Many circles. It has been difficult to distinguish death from birth, endings from beginnings. I have left traces of myself: eggs, spheres of possibility. I have come to respect the unborn in me, the question, the not-yet realized, the hope. In the depth of the self, at the intersection of "was" with "will be," is my beginning. The place of birth. The source of infinite possibility. Here is all I will never actualize. I have sometimes believed there was not time, or I could not summon the courage, or master the skills, or raise the enthusiasm. Sometimes I have lost hold, and all has slipped away. Sometimes I have failed. It does not matter. Nothing is lost. There is no blame. I can go home. I can go where I was born, to the place of all my beginnings. I can go into my deepest self where anything is possible. I go there and rejoice in who I am, who I have become. I lay down the unfulfilled hopes. I lay down the possibilities I never chose to actualize. I lay them down like eggs in a warm and nourishing place. They have their own becoming. I let them go. I rest.

The beautiful silver and blue creature
Lay close to the river's edge,
And the stone lay within her.

The treasure is here. I stare into the river. I am lost in the wonder of water, the hope of tomorrow, the thrill of seeing at last the Within. I believe the treasure is here, the stone, the precise point of being that is everything. I sit still. I let the quiet wash me. Here the current is imperceptible. I do not see, not yet. The treasure that is here hides. I will find it. I will recognize. If I sit still enough, if I breathe deeply, if I live in awareness, the density that encloses the treasure will fall away, and it will be released. It is truth. It is the power of connection with my origins. It is what continues.

Her life was complete, and so she died.

"Complete" and "tidy" are different. Death almost always leaves me with loose ends and jagged edges. All kinds of death do this: everyday deaths, like moving from one town to another, changing jobs or careers, watching children leave home to create their own lives; and that ultimate death—it is hardly ever tidy. There is a new grandchild never to be seen. There is a home just purchased, the boxes not even unpacked. There is a wedding in two weeks, or a child still in school, or a newly married spouse, or a pile of bills, or a book half written. The two ends of an event, or of a life, come together in a circle. Completions. What is within the circle is whole. What is outside continues to struggle and to grow. I can let it go gratefully.

She became part of the river.
Her flesh became food for a mother bear and her cubs.
Her bones settled into the river bed,
Enriching the land.

I seem separate only for a while. There is a pattern in my cells that is the pattern of the universe, a flowing in and through all being, and I am part of it. "You are earth," the Creator tells the first people, "and you shall return to earth." I bring to awareness a bit of matter I call "self." My task here is conscious connection with all creation. There is no "other." We are continuous. The river and I are one, and this is compassion. There is no real distance between me and the woman and her child starving in Africa, or on the streets of New York. We are one life, one being. I am food for her. Not only do I not have a right to withhold myself, I simply cannot. I do not have the power. Everything I am is shared.

The beautiful silver and blue creature
Became part of all creatures
And of the river bed where she had been born.
And she freed the jagged stone
Into the tumbling waters of the mountain river.

Out of every loss something remains. Something goes on. Something
continues to give life. Something is set free. Maybe it is the essence of
what is past. Maybe it is the seed of the future. It was a mistake of
youthful years to suppose I could pick up something or someone, wrap
my life around that one, even for a short time, and not be marked
forever by a presence. Everything I harbor in my heart changes me.
Even when I set it free, it accompanies me. It carries my spirit beyond
itself. Even memory is not necessary. Everything I am bears witness.

For a thousand years
The jagged stone tumbled down the river
Toward the cold blue sea.

I continue. I walk the beaches and the sheer edges of rock by mountain streams. I sit in the shade of trees older than my dreams. Today a particular stone, granite-shaped like an egg, beckons to me. I want it for its history. I want it for its antiquity. I want it because of the unimaginable time it must have taken to arrive here, on the river bank, so close to the ocean. I want it because, being an egg-like stone, it reminds me of Mother Earth, of continuance, and of hope. I keep it for remembrance and for courage. I keep it to remind myself to continue.

The waters lifted her up,
Dropped her into pools
Where she whirled for years round and round,
Becoming smooth,
Becoming smaller as her rough edges dissolved.

I am placed here. I do not choose my community or family the way I choose my friends. The stone collector bends and picks a stone up from the road—or the beach or the field—because in that stone is something unique that catches her eye. She drops the stone into her pouch with the others. It does not necessarily fit. Some of the stones have sharp edges, and they grind against one another as the stone collector walks. Sometimes, in meditative moments—watching the fire or the stars—the collector takes her pouch and rolls the stones around in her hand. The friction chips rough edges, creates new contours. Sometimes she takes one stone out, one she has had for years, and polishes it, and the oil on her fingers makes it shine. It takes years, and much tumbling around within the stone collector's pouch, to become smooth. I am like the stone. In the end, when the stone collector takes me out and polishes me and holds me up to the sun, and I feel the warmth and light of the sun pass into and through me, then I will rejoice. Over many years, through conflicts past counting, through disappointments and confusion, I have endured and will endure until, at last, I will become round and smooth, clear and complete.

Then she lay for a hundred years
Where the water was still,
Where the sun warmed her in summer,
And where, during the long winters,
Ice enclosed her
As if she and the water had become one thing.

Being is still. I sit staring into the fireplace. I watch snow fall. I listen to the rain. I get up each day and fix meals and wash clothes and go to work and come home and watch the news, and each day is like the one before. This is not depression. Depression feels like nausea, suffocation, being buried alive. This is stillness. Our culture dislikes stillness. Move! Get things done! We need new ideas, a new place to go, a new fashion to wear, a new car, a new project. We have to get somewhere. "What's wrong?" friends wonder when I am still. "Get moving," they caution. "Life will pass you by." But there are times when I simply *am* life. There are moments, days, months—sometimes years—of simply being. I spend a season watching tiny, sticky leaves unfold to the sun, watching children open to their unique and unrepeatable lives. And while I watch, I feel the whole world inside me, in a place so still that every vibration of being ripples there. It is a place where the water and I are one.

At last she was picked up
In the beak of a bird,
Who thought she was perhaps a clam,
And dropped back into the current
To continue her journey home to the cold blue sea.

Life takes sudden turns. I cannot predict it. It startles me. The most unexpected thing can move me. I am picked up. Suddenly I am flying! Plummeting! Whisked into the current. Birth can do it, or death of a loved one. I turn around in the grocery line and a woman smiles; I feel I have known her forever, but I have never seen her before. We talk. We have coffee. By evening, my mind and heart are speeding off in a direction I have never gone before. Or I sit in my favorite chair reading a magazine when the telephone rings. They have decided to publish my book, or my son is shipping out to war, or the child down the street is lost and her parents need help. Then I am up and running. Almost before I know it, my life is changed. This is not to say I have no control over what I do. The decision, always, belongs to me. But I am part of a pattern, an evolution. My stillness prepares me to be lifted up by life and to experience what needs doing next. My decision to act or not to act, to move with life or to remain still, creates me, makes me who I am, takes me home.

She learned the wisdom of the river,
Which was called
"Endure."

Endurance is like a river. There have been times I gritted my teeth, determined to get through whatever life has dealt. Endurance is not like that. People break when they are too hard. Endurance is liquid. Endurance is a flood of tears at a rejection I think I cannot bear, and then through my tears, I notice the moon washed in a brilliance that expands my heart. The next morning I begin again. Endurance is a flowing that never ceases. It surrounds obstacles, it washes them away, or it dissolves them. Endurance is the deep flow under the ice of winter. Endurance is the shallow flow continuing through years of drought, carving rivulets through clay. Endurance sculpts the canyon and the gorge. It reveals every stratum of existence. It uncovers lost and buried beauty.

She learned the wisdom of the sun,
Which was called
"Receive."

Wisdom speaks. Her sound is of wind and of the sun's dance on the river: "Receive the golden grain. Take it into your storehouse. Grind it. Make bread and be nourished. Receive the day. Rejoice in the slow wash of rose at the horizon. Receive the sight of trees leaning, distinct against the light. Receive the first bird's song. Set out. Walk toward the morning. Breathe in the sunlight. Take it in through eyes and nose and skin. Let it make your hair shine. Receive also the sheltered sun, the sun behind clouds, the sun eclipsed, the sun setting. Receive the shadow. Receive, too, the sun that burns, the scorching sun, the sun that dries the land, that turns the land to sand, drifting. Learn to survive on the water stored in the tough stems of desert plants, in the fibrous roots. Receive both the light and the shadow the sun creates. And when clouds cover the sun, receive the blessing of rain. For what you receive is not always to your liking; it is, instead, for your growth, for your transformation. And your teacher of life is often also your initiator into the mysteries of death."

The wisdom of a thousand winters
was called
"Wait."

Waiting is an attitude toward the future. It is not immobility. Waiting respects life's rhythm. It does not push. It does not insist. It is like the story of watching a butterfly emerge from a chrysalis. "Ah," I think, "this is too much pain, too slow; I'll just help a bit." Gently, carefully I peel the soft shell away from the fragile wings until the delicate creature lies, still crumpled, in my palm. I hum to it, a lullaby. I pray, "Please, please live, open your wings. You were meant for air, for the sky." But the butterfly dies. It needed more time.

So I wait. And the waiting is filled with activities of life: weather-stripping windows, calling AAA to jump-start the car, cuddling by the fireplace wrapped in a goose-down comforter, ice-skating on a frozen lake, building a snowman, walking under frost-covered trees and feeling the skin on my face stiffen with the cold, sitting by the window watching snow fall. In March, when I can smell springtime, it snows again, as much as thirty-six inches in one storm, and everyone is tired of snow. But I shovel it from the sidewalk, and life continues, and I wait.

The wisdom of the mountain
With its trees, its bears,
Its birds and wild flowers,
Was called
"Continue."

Life will not be stopped. Sometimes I feel like rock, or like a tree that has pulled up minerals from the ground and petrified. Fear does this. Cold anger does it, too. I resist. I do not want to go on. I want a hardness that protects from pain. But the hardness does not last. It cannot. My rigid earth quakes. Cracks form. Birds drop seeds that lodge in me and drink the rain. They grow. I am covered in green. Wild flowers rise toward the sun. I am suddenly soft. It is my nature to continue.

And the wisdom of the beautiful silver and blue creature,
Who brought her to the mountain in the first place
And released her to the river
Where she could return to the cold blue sea,
Was called
"Come Home."

Everything is changing. The house where I grew up is sold and redesigned. My friends have moved away or are strangers with vaguely familiar faces. The new people do not know my name. I cannot go home. I really cannot. I can only *come* home to my true self. And that, I do. I must. Coming home is a re-turn. It is a turn toward life. It is a re-incorporation of all that is before with what is now. It brings the past—and the people, places, and experiences of the past—into a meaningful pattern with the present. It is an act of soul, an acceptance of all life: the suffering and the joy—and the changes. Coming home is an act of forgiveness and an act of hope.

At last one spring,
When the snow on the mountain had been deep
And heavy rains blew in from the sea,
The river flooded to a torrent.

Ecstasy is pure gift. It can happen to anyone. Suddenly all the conditions are present for flood. The flow of life increases and becomes so strong, it is impossible to ignore. It can be pain; it can be joy; probably both are flowing in and out of one another. Rising. Rising. Everything is alive. My heart is bursting. I feel every breath. The top of my head tingles. My fingertips throb as though springs of fresh water might flow from them. My eyes are pools. They reflect the world. I hold my breath. I realize I am a channel for God. The flood bursts through me, taking trees in its turbulence, lifting boulders, cutting at the shoreline, depositing silt, creating islands where before was clear water. I am powerless against it. I do not want it to stop. I cry out. I rejoice. I gasp in sheer awe.

It swept down the mountain;
It tore trees out of the earth;
It picked up rocks as large as bears.

Life is more than can be controlled. It is a torrent. Torrents fill me with awe. I saw my first tornado when I was four years old. It hung over the lake, a grey tail whipping back and forth. It picked up fishing boats, dashing them onto the beach. It broke in a waterfall of rain. I have seen floods and blizzards, stood in blinding desert sun, been slashed by wind-driven sand. There are torrents in my soul: torrents of tears, torrents of joy, torrents that rip and tear and dissolve; torrents that pick me up, turn me around, and set me in a place I have never seen before. I stutter. I cry out. I bend and kneel in the dust. There is a violence in it—a violence and a mercy. I deserve neither. This is not a matter of deserving. The torrent *is*. I live with it. I live in it.

It lifted the stone
From where she was wedged
Between two roots of an aspen tree
And whirled her into the torrent.

A turn of the head, and everything changes. Someone dies. A friend goes on vacation and never returns. I leave work one day and know I cannot keep doing the same thing every day for twenty more years. It is time now to buy that craft shop, write that book, study archaeology, save the rain forests.

I feel cracked open, raw. I feel pulled up by the roots. I feel I have to go, I have to do it—whatever *it* is. A week ago I would have said, impossible. Then life turned, and now everything in me rushes toward it, drawn by an inexplicable love for all I could be, of all I had ever hoped to realize.

The river carried her to where it crashed
Against the powerful, curling waves
Of the cold blue sea
And dropped her on a white beach.

Conflict is the mind's torrent. I stand where the river empties into the ocean and watch the tumult at the point of contact. The river runs wide toward her mouth and lingers behind the large sand dune, almost a peninsula, formed against the sea. Anglers cast their lines, and pelicans gather, dive, rise, disperse with their catch. At her mouth the rocks are teeth. Cliffs jut out, and the ocean licks, sucks, pounds the resisting stone. River and ocean meet in walls of water breaking and falling against each other. Opposing currents. Fresh water and salt. Everlasting conflict. My mind gets caught like that, with opposites crashing. What to do? How to be? This or that? Either, or? Am I right or is he? Endlessly. I lie awake, waves of opposites relentless in my mind. Sometime after midnight, Mercy drops out from the tumult and rests against my heart. Mercy toward the river, mercy toward the sea. Mercy toward myself who contains both, who lives with and through conflict but is not limited by it. Mercy toward being, itself, immense ocean, endless river, where opposites merge.

There she lay among other stones,
Stones of every color,
Stones from the mountain and stones from the sea,
Together,
Rolling with the tides,
Touching one another,
Whispering in the language land and sea speak when they meet.

Diversity enriches. I want a world of color, sparkling, where differences develop soul, give resonance to life. Where northern European heritage, white, first-second-third generation immigrants live with Chippewa or Sioux. Where the German and the Irish mix. Where French folk attend a church dedicated to Our Lady of Guadelupe, and the Dutch are dancing a "Mbaqanga" beat. I want to sing with them, and dance. My mind needs stretching. My feelings require that touch of difference. My understanding increases under the pressure of cultural dissonance. It is the same whisper the many-colored stones make rolling against each other. It is the sound land and sea make when they meet. It is the language of the world.

The gleaming stone,
Which now was smooth and round,
Whispered on the shore of the cold blue sea
For another thousand years.

Transformation happens in an instant or a lifetime. It cannot be planned. St. Teresa of Avila lived twenty-five years in a darkness of the soul, in the absence of her God. Then, suddenly, God's light flooded her. Probably it was a day like any other. Probably she was doing all the usual things. Getting up at five a.m., taking care of convent business, praying as best she could. Then, suddenly, God.

Grief is like that. Self-awareness, too. I have no end to the tears I cry for what is lost: my childhood, my innocence, my possibilities, the people I love. I cannot begin to plumb the depth of memory, the vast scope of all I have hidden from my heart. What was once hidden now whispers in my dreams. Self-deception drops away like scales. In an instant. In a lifetime. When or how I am transformed does not matter. Transformation while I work. Transformation while I am talking with a friend. Transformation happens when I am devoted to what is in front of me, each moment. It happens when the sea swells in me and, deep in my heart, keeps on whispering.

Often the sea swept her deep into its waters,
But always she returned to the white sands
Where the summer sun warmed her
And the winter rains washed her clean.

Life achieves balance when I do not resist it. Heart balances mind. I learn the connections: the depth with the surface, suffering with peace, loss with joy, solitude with social intercourse. The balance is seldom fifty-fifty. I balance according to my need. There are people who need fifteen days in the sea's depths to every one day on the beach. Fifteen to one: that is their balance point. Comparisons are futile; each is unique. I feel my way. When I have enough of depth, I am tossed upon the sand. When I accept being alone, someone comes.

Coastal winds brushed her with sand,
Polishing her,
Until she was not only smooth but translucent.

Only the clear see clearly. The pure of heart see God. I once knew a translucent person, an old nun, thin as an altar candle, eyes like flames. She was completely clear; she harbored no lie. And the lies in me? She saw right through them. She made me feel like water. She could see to the bottom. I could not have hidden myself from her; I did not try; I did not want to. Only the old ones can be pure. Only the ones over whom the sands of life have passed a thousand times, sands driven by rain, sands heavy with the sea, sharp sands, the many-sided crystals. They wear us down. They change our shape. Finally, only the soul remains, round, bright, clear, and shining in our eyes.

Now, when the sun shone down on her,
She was filled with light.

Resistance is a habit of fear. I have ways of resisting Light that are so subtle, I swear I have not caused my own blindness. "I can't" is one way; "I am not worthy" is another. I am certain I tell the truth. "Vision is for the artists and the saints," I mumble. "I'm more ordinary than that. I do my best. I survive. Maybe I can't expect more." But even in my mumbling, I feel a barely perceptible turn of heart toward the possibility of grace. When a loss is devastating, I start to hold my breath against each moment as it comes. Breathing no longer feels natural. My stomach tightens around my spirit. I begin to fear again that there is no life on the other side of grief. But only the slightest turn from fear to hope, and the moment becomes light. I can breathe it in, an inhalation of spirit. I learn that everything is grace.

She learned the wisdom of the wind,
Which was called
"Flow."

Opposites seek balance. Wind rises sheer and unexpected. The maple leaves let go, whirl, fly, a mess of crimson birds. Oak and elm leaves lift from where they fell to the ground some days ago. Small tornadoes of gold and brown. The flow between hot and cold air. The filling of a vacuum. A balance of energies. I need to keep the passages open between opposites. I do not do myself any favor by trying to be too responsible, too perfect.

Whenever I concentrate on anything to its extreme, suddenly its opposite comes nipping at my heels; or worse, consumes my life. Compulsions of all kinds are attempts to cancel out opposites. I want to feel good constantly. But the opposite rushes in, often destructively, and I am left with pain. Then I feel so fooled, so shamed.

When I allow the wind to flow, I feel everything there is of life. Joy and pain. Responsibility and play—including a bit of mischief now and then. Work and rest. Communion and solitude.

The wisdom of the sand,
Called
"Change."

What am I, really? In this moment? Through my lifetime? A glass blower rolls his long wand in molten glass until it forms a sphere of liquid fire, and then he blows. The sphere becomes a globe. He blows again; he forms the globe into a pitcher; he cuts it loose. A few moments, only, from molten glass to crystal. Once, it had been sand. Before sand, what? Rock from earth's center combined with the shards of a trillion shells, all subjected to the transforming fire and breath? Changed. Immediately. Fundamentally. But sand is also changed from day to day by wind and tides, slowly, subtlety, almost imperceptibly, but certainly. So is everything. So am I.

The wisdom of the stars,
Called
"Shine."

The soul is endless. I try to fathom the night sky. It is the dark of the moon. A bonfire throws sparks upward. I lie on my back and stare at the dizzying array hanging in the infinite darkness. The small, contained light of the bonfire magnifies the vastness into which I gaze. Its showers of sparks cannot reach even to the tops of the pines. The starlight shines clear from a distance not measurable in space so much as in time—hundreds and thousands of years of light away, and still seen, still clear, still shining. Human shining transcends reason and imagination; it goes beyond death. I look at the night sky, and what I see reflects my soul. Infinite capacity. A shining of spirit measured in endless light.

And the wisdom of the tides,
Called
"Remember."

Nothing I have ever been is lost to me. It rises like the tide in the glow of remembering. I hold it all in my heart. It is a moonstone, subtle, shimmering with all my life. My childhood is there in laughter and in tears. A bird's egg broken in my hand. A lullaby to take away my fear. Every hurt and every shout, my whispers, whimpering, and song. Every failure, every glory of my youth is there. My loves are there. I look into their eyes. And those I felt as enemies, from whom I learned my strength and my integrity, all of them are there. The deaths are there, the births, the promises and broken promises, every healing word and touch, every smile. The tides call forth all that is deep in me: the essence of myself. The waters carry it ashore. Wisdom remembers, accepts, lets all of it flow and ebb and flow again. Wisdom shimmers in it all like the moon on the midnight tides. Wisdom gleans from everything.

One day after a thousand years,
A girl-child came to the white beach
By the cold blue sea.

Some changes are quantum. Some moments, more powerful than others, set me apart: a girl-child on the beach, someone both evolving and participating in creation's evolution. My first word. My first song. My first act of generosity. Each act expands my consciousness. Each act enlarges my soul. And every subsequent action throughout life increases my individuality. Each of us walks the beach, bends, and picks up a solitary stone to carry all her days. Each one of us is set apart, unique, separate, and alone. Yet each contains all. Each is continuous with all. Every movement anywhere affects each one. Each one affects the world.

She belonged to a tribe called the People.

Earth is my tribe. It has no boundaries. Its people are everywhere. Race is not a factor and neither is ethnicity, gender, religious belief, political affiliation, economic status, education, or age. There is enormous diversity among the members of our tribe, yet we seem able to recognize each other while still strangers. Perhaps we see a particular quality of hope and of compassion. Perhaps we recognize a love for the earth and all its creatures that encourages even the smallest and most insignificant of us to survive and flourish. The earth people sing a lot and laugh good and loud, and with enormous joy. We weep, too, in the presence of suffering, as well as in the presence of beauty. The earth people wander the land and seas, and when two of us meet, we tell stories and sing songs, we light candles, bless bread, and read poems to each other. Then we go on our way because there is healing to attend to, and teaching, and works of justice and mercy.

She had long hair the color of a raven's wing
And eyes like black obsidian.
Her skin was the color of a well-oiled myrtle wood bowl.

Unique beauty is the splendor of being. I watch a woman take the pins from her hair and let it tumble down her back. It is the color of ripe wheat at noon. She lifts her arms. She dances. Her feet are bare against the grass. She is liquid. She is fresh, poured milk. She bends. She is a daisy in the wind. I see another whose skin is chestnut brown and smooth. Her fine hands float over the piano keys like swallow wings. She plays Debussy. She plays Rachmaninoff. She comes down hard and her fingers prance. She tosses her curly hair. I know a girl, a copper-toned reed growing from a crack in the granite on an island in the lake. She makes soft music with an on-shore breeze. I know these people and their reflections. I see because I love. If I could love myself as well, what might I see in me?

The girl-child's name was Shell
Because she gathered food from the sea
To nourish her People.

I bear many names. I name myself, and I am named by others. My parents named me at birth with the name spoken in their hearts. I have a name passed down through generations. I am named out of the memories of my people. I am named because of their needs. I am named according to what I do and who I show myself to be. I bear pet names, nicknames, secret names. There are names my lover speaks in the stillness of the night. Names spoken in a sigh, in giggles, in anger, and in pain. I bear the names of my dreams, of hopes, of all I imagine I could become. I call myself these names in the silver morning while dawn shines the mist. I whisper these names into the ocean's roar. I am many and I am one. I am myself.

Shell listened to the land talking with the sea.
In their language of whispers,
She thought she could hear her own breath,
The beating of her own heart,
The sound made by her blood as it traveled through her body.

All things breathe with a single breath. When I am still, I hear the connections, sense the oneness of creation. I cannot think my way through to this kind of hearing; it is not a belief. I cannot will it; it is not a goal. I cannot even search for it; it is not outside me. It is revelation. In an instant everything is known, everything is loved—the past, the future, the present—all in the same moment. I am all right. I am no longer afraid to die. Inside and outside do not matter anymore; they do not even exist. Nothing is separate—not the mountain, not the ocean, not the stars, not God. All things exist together as one.

As she walked in the white sand,
She watched gulls riding the wind.
And far out in the cold blue sea,
She noticed a spray of water
Caused by her brother the whale.

When my soul is open, I see. I see my brothers, the whales. I see my sons and daughters, the children of the planet. I see my sisters, the birds; my mothers, the mountains; my fathers, the trees. They tell me who I am.

There is a story about St. Augustine. He was walking on a beach next to the ocean, pondering the immensity of God. All at once he noticed a little child playing in the sand. The child had dug a hole and was running back and forth from the waves with a thimble, pouring water from the ocean into the hole.

"What are you doing?" questioned Augustine.

"I am going to put the ocean into the hole I made," the boy replied.

"My dear boy," Augustine laughed, "you can't do that. Can't you see that the ocean is immense, and your hole is so very small?"

"And can't you see," the boy gazed at the man, "that the mystery of God is larger than your mind?" Then the boy disappeared.

Instantly Augustine *did* comprehend. It was not theory he comprehended. It was not theology. It was the experience of God. He had opened his soul.

Shell also watched where her feet walked
For signs of crabs dug into the sand
And places where clams hid.

I seek out the hidden. I sit quietly and let it appear. The hidden
memories will appear. The hidden loves and fears and hopes, all of
them will appear. I am still. I watch. So much is hidden every day. So
much crawls underground. These things seek the dark places. I am
still, and I watch my dreams. I watch what happens when I gaze at the
stars or when the sun melts the sky at evening, smoky rose, the color
of fires that are burning themselves out. I watch inside my eyes, inside
my mind. I feel the memories with my heart and in my belly. I am an
ancient jar, a clay bowl, a porcelain ginger pot; covered. I contain the
memories of all life. Each memory is connected to the memories of
the universe. Every love is one with universal love. My fears are not
different from the fears of the fledgling eagle clinging to the cliff's edge,
beckoned by the sky. My rage is the rage of volcanoes contained,
boiling, ready to erupt. My abandon is of oceans and mountain
streams. Nothing I contain is not known. It comes out of hiding. I see
myself. I let myself be.

Suddenly Shell noticed a beautiful stone,
One that seemed to shine
As though the light of the sun lived within it.

Light penetrates any darkness. There are times, earth-shaking, soul-shattering times, when I feel at the end of my life. I am going along, doing my work, living my life, thinking I am fine, in the right place, being who I am. Suddenly my life falls like rain all around me. I am no longer at peace with myself. My stomach churns constantly. I nibble at food and nothing tastes good. I lose weight. I cannot concentrate on my work. I withdraw from friends. I try to act as if nothing were wrong. I push myself, hard, to appear normal. Constantly my mind turns over options, trying to find how to live. I am afraid to change. If I do that, I reason, I will be no one. Nothing. But the old life feels like nothing, too. One night I tell myself my life is worth nothing. I think about dying. But the effort of thought is too much. I go to bed. It is a night that passes in an instant. I seem to close my eyes and open them immediately to the morning and the song of birds. Very distinctly I hear the words, "I Am." I am not dead. I am alive. I does not matter whether I stay as I am or I change. Whatever I do, I am. Wherever life is, there is light.

She bent to pick it up.

To everything of importance in life, I must bend. The child. The garden. The lover. Even if I need not bend physically, I bend my heart, my mind, my spirit. I bend to knowledge, to mystery, to beauty. I bend to suffering, to the inexplicable. I bend to the teacher, to the healer, to the pure of heart. I bend before birth and before death. I bend with tears and with an expanding heart. I bend even in the face of evil. What else can I do? I touch my forehead to the ground. I cry out. I cry, "God!" I bend when I am powerful and when I am devoid of power. Reverence is how I discover the nature of things. Simplicity is the way I accept.

The stone felt more smooth than the softest deerskin,
And it was round as the full moon.

Living takes time. Time to taste. Time to touch. Time to notice what is present in each moment. Living takes awareness, the willingness to be focused now, in the moment. When I dwell on the past with regret, I am not aware. When I worry about the future, I displace myself in time, and the only life I can live slips away unnoticed.

But some things I cannot forget. Some things from the past enrich my life. They are as much a part of me as my own heart, as my breath. I cannot forget the softness of my mother's cheek against my hands; the rich, black earth sifting through my fingers in the spring; the sound of rain at the moment of a death. I cannot forget because I live these things, completely present to them, and they merge with my cells. I remember them in my fingers and in the spiral chambers of bone that form my inner ear. I am more myself with them than without them.

She held it to her forehead
And then to the base of her throat,
And it was warm.

Feeling warms me. Cold as a stone, that is how people talk about people without feeling. That is how people talk about the dead. But life is warm. Hot sand on a beach. Log fire blazing when outside the rains come, when snow falls. Sun-soaked gravel roads. Tanned skin of a child playing in summer fields. Warmth of human touch. In my thought center and my word center, I need warmth. Cold analysis, cold objectivity—there is something false about these things, something dead. When my thoughts absorb light, they are warm. When my words express the connection of mind with heart, they are warm. Warmth heals. Warmth expresses itself in tenderness. Warmth gives life.

This was the kind of stone her People called
"Finding Stone"
Because whatever you needed in order to live,
If you wore this stone,
You would find the needed thing.

The best things in life come as a surprise. Most of the time I have not known until after something comes to me that I needed it in order to live. I set out to look for what I need, but something else finds me. Perhaps it is not belief I need so much as readiness. What I call belief often makes me blind. I cannot see the truth; I think I need something else. What I really need is an open heart. Eyes that see beyond the expected. Hands willing to explore the unacceptable. When I stand ready with an open heart, I find that even God is a surprise, not what I expected, not at all. Opening to the surprise of God, I find everything I need for life.

Shell closed her hand around the smooth round stone
And thanked the Earth Spirit
Who had brought her together with this Finding Stone.

Life is a spiral of gratitude. Gratitude keeps things going, expanding, evolving, becoming. Ocean, forest, mountain, desert, the lakes and rivers, bears and birds, the cricket singing through the night—all things express gratitude in being fully what they are. They live and die with abandon, with hearts open to the fullness of earth of which they are part. Only we humans tighten our hearts like stone fists. Only we humans grasp our small lives to ourselves in an attempt to preserve ourselves, to keep ourselves from harm and death, to isolate ourselves, to insist we are sufficient to ourselves. Only we humans refuse to participate in the spiral of gratitude. I do not want to refuse. I want to hold life lightly in my hand. If it wants to overflow, I will let it. If it wants to be given again and again, I will give it. I did not create myself, and I am not limited to my personal boundaries. I am, myself, earth's gratitude.

Shell thanked her Finding Stone
For all the years the stone had traveled toward her
And all the hardships the stone had endured
In order to arrive here,
On this white beach
Beside this cold blue sea,
On this very day that Shell had come from her village
To find food for her People.

Loss creates space for the miracle that makes me whole. I am open, living from moment to moment, seeing only what is in front of me, too emptied to desire anything but being. Suddenly the connecting link is right in front of me. It is called synchronicity, that amazing coincidence when two seemingly unrelated events collide, setting off an explosion in my mind, quickening my heart, changing my life. What I had felt as loss was the clearing of anything that impeded the miracle. It was the making ready. My entire life has brought me to this place, this time. I open my arms. I expand my heart. I am full. I am whole.

Around her neck, Shell wore a small leather pouch.

Signs are all around us. Talismans. Symbols of transformation. I have an heirloom ring that has survived every loss, every death. It connects me to my past, to an existence before my birth, before the birth of my mother when she swam in her own mother's womb, when the egg that would someday open into me had already begun to form in her ovaries, when I was present in my grandmother's womb, a pinpoint of life, a facet of diamond. It teaches me that I am not alone. My life is joined to others by common and by mystic things, by stones and by words in diaries, by carved ivory combs, a silver cup, a wedding ring. Things old and new. A golden feather dropped in a field. A pottery shard. An arrowhead. I am joined to people and to nature. I am joined to God.

Because she was still a girl,
The leather pouch was new
And still empty.

All life is a beginning. I need an open, spontaneous, joyful attitude that knows it does not know. I need the emptiness in me. It is the wide-eyed child. As a child, I gasped when the snowflake disappeared under my careful touch. I did not know what a snowflake was. When I grew up, I was no longer surprised by melting snowflakes. I thought I knew what they were. But I do not. When I think I understand the leaf, the river, the seasons, my friend, myself, I do not understand. I need to find the part in my soul still empty, still able to be surprised, still open to wonder. I need to treasure that space, protect it, see life through it—unimpeded. I need a beginner's mind.

When her grandmother had given it to her
As a gift
For her twelfth winter,
She had called it a medicine pouch.

Transition times are sacred times. Birth, menarche, maternity, menopause, death: I know them. I seek the circle of community for support because transitions separate me from the familiar and leave me feeling alone. The girl comes together with the grandmother sharing stories, the mothers share children, the widows hold one another and, weeping, dance their sorrow. During these times, I reach deep, as though my life were a medicine bag that contains the secrets of healing. I need wisdom to know how to use what the medicine bag contains. Sometimes emptiness, itself, is the secret. Other times, choice: the rosemary or the sage? The amethyst or the turquoise? Tears? Rest? Laughter? Shall I dance or walk along the beach? Shall I be alone or seek a friend's embrace? At least once in life, the answer is to open the medicine pouch, pour it out, all of it, give it all away. I already contain everything I need to be healed.

Grandmother had told Shell
That the pouch must remain empty
Until something from the earth
Called to Shell
With the voice of healing, wisdom, and power.

It could have been anything. It happened to be a stone. It could have been a broken shell or a piece of seaweed. It could have been a tree fallen across her path, a thicket of roses, a bird with a wounded wing. It could have been a child digging in the mud, an old man, a sick woman, a person with nothing to eat. It could have been a rabbit, trapped, or a soaring hawk. It is the call that makes the difference. What is the call I hear, and in what chamber of my soul does it echo? The world has so much noise. I listen through the tumult of the world to the voice of the earth. If all I hear is noise, I am are not listening deeply enough. What I take in is what I will become.

"It may be any of the colors of the rainbow
And must contain the light of the sun,"
Grandmother had said.

The healing way is the way of light. Whatever in me is opaque, whatever resists light, whatever is closed, tight, rejecting; whatever refuses hope, tenderness, wonder, and spontaneity—this is the barrier to my healing. The Finding Stone is earth in all her multiplicity, containing light in full spectrum. I am healed when I see the star at midnight and can stand full in the sun of midday. I am healed when I open my heart to the incredible, to the realization that healing is possible and as natural as light in the stone polished to translucence by the sands and by the sea.

It must have come through fire.

The powers of healing are purified by fire. I bring them to mind, the fires in my life. I remember them. I name them, each one. They are the moments that consume, that transform, that cast a glow on the world to make it new. They are moments of terror; they are moments of ecstasy. They are moments of total loss and absolute creation. I say the moments aloud, a litany. With my voice chant the voices of many: "My loved one died. He was killed in a war—she was killed on the highway—he was killed in the field he plowed—she was killed by cancer. I lost my child—I lost her to drugs—I lost her to misunderstanding—I lost her to the future. I never bore a child and that is the fire—I bore seven children and that is the fire—I left my childhood home and wandered all my life; the earth became my dwelling and that is the fire—I lived my entire life on an inland farm; I never saw the ocean or a mountain; I watched an oak tree grow from a seed, and from its branches hangs a swing for my grandchildren and that is the fire." Each flame distills to essence. Each of us stands in a brightness that reveals the soul. In each memory we are purified.

It must have spoken with the waves.

Waves call me to my origins. They are the waves of my blood; the waves of my breath, my thoughts, my emotions; the cycles of my creations; the tides of sleep and waking, of my watery dreams. Waves bear me up and whisper in my heart the secrets of my beginnings. I listen. I practice listening. I attend to the waves of breath and blood. I learn to distinguish nuances of ebb and flow. River waves take one direction: they rush; they are white water down mountains; they uproot trees and roll boulders. The waves of lakes are barely audible: they lap against reeds along the shore; storms churn them into foam; morning smoothes them with mist inside of which the white egret stands motionless. Ocean waves swell into walls: they are thick, powerful; they break against the rocks with thunder. The ocean is mother of us all. I see her in dreams, coming through mist, the divine mist, rising from the original waters. She rises, star of the sea, fullness of love, as divine as anything I can fathom. I listen. She calls me by name.

It must have listened to the music of the wind.

In the heart of each, I hear the music of all. I listen to the wind rustle the leaves of the cottonwood tree. It calms me. But calm is not the only song wind sings. Tornado, hurricane, cyclone; wind bringing the blizzard; wind fanning the flames of forest fires; wind lifting the ocean's waves, twisting trees, roaring over earth, ripping vines, flattening fields of grain—these winds also sing. It is said that God speaks only in the gentle breeze. That is untrue. Spirita Sancta is the wind of God. She clears a space in my mind. She blows as hard as need be. She sweeps through, uprooting dead thoughts. She whirls into my heart, awakening me to symphonic complexity. She thunders and she roars. She takes my breath away. She blows new life into me like a whirlwind. She is in me and around me. I think I can fly on her. I lift my soul. I cry out. I sing.

Shell opened her leather medicine pouch,
And into it she put the round clear stone.

I learn to recognize what to keep. I keep what is of value, what nurtures and transforms. A pearl of great price, the Bible calls it. A medicine pouch is small; it will not hold much. I need to discriminate. Choose wisely. Someone found a treasure buried in a field, the Bible says, and he sold everything he had and bought that field. Some treasures surpass everything else life offers. I keep them in my heart. They change my life. They work miracles. I become the treasure I hold.

Then she gathered food.

I gather food of every kind. Food for the heart and mind. Food for the soul. Food to make the body strong, to make the body supple, to fill the body with energy for work, for play, for love. I gather food that is good: nuts and grains and flowers that can be eaten. I gather the leaves of plants that heal. I gather roots. I gather the ripe fruit. I gather beautiful food: the song of the people at morning, the smiles of lovers, children at play, works of the poet and painter and sculptor and composer, works of the farmer and inventor and scientist and those who sail on the sea. I gather the food of the gods: the food of prayer, of silence, of awe before the mystery of being. I gather food and fill the baskets of life to overflowing. I gather food and live from it. It brings me through sorrow, and I am not crushed; it is a store for when times are lean and the land lies barren. I can feed the hungry, and we will survive. The food I gather now is a promise for the years to come.

Before the sun was at its high point in the sky,
Her basket was filled with shellfish,
And she was walking through the tall trees
Toward the camp of her People.

The return home comes at the moment of fullness. This is the spiral of life. This is the law of the universe. The empty will be filled. I go out empty. I am the space of possibility. I am a blank page, an open hand, a song that has no words. I search the earth. I gather what is available. I turn toward home, bringing the gift that fills my heart. I have become the fullness. I am the gift.

Shell lived eighty summers and eighty winters after that day
And always,
Day and night,
She wore the medicine pouch that held her Finding Stone.

My life rises from a central and enduring core. What is there, precious enough, to hold in my heart for eighty years? What can I not live without? What is strong enough to endure the challenges life brings? What is steady enough to survive intact through every change? What is there with the depth, the density, the purity, the brilliance to make me want to preserve it even at the cost of my life? What is, at the same time, so common, so ordinary, so natural that it warms my heart and gives peace to my mind? This is my Finding Stone.

Shell grew to be beautiful and wise
And honored by her People.

Beauty, wisdom, and honor grow out of fidelity. All beauty in the popular culture seems to looks alike; it is hard to tell one beauty queen from another. But beauty is unique. Beauty in nature stuns me with its variety. The giant cedar never will become a rose. The hummingbird is not the bear. When I see my essence and am faithful to it, I become the promise of my vision. I see as no one else sees. I work to create what I see. I shape it in good form. My fidelity grows. When I am young, the content of my vision tells me what is good. When I grow old, my vision expands to see the beauty in all. Wisdom grows. I honor the beauty that marks its presence in everything.

When the People were hungry,
she found food.

There comes a time when the focus of life turns from myself, outward. I learn I cannot "find myself," I simply am. I discover that self-actualization is never an act directed toward the self. Instead, it is the self acting on behalf of the people, on behalf of the world. Is a child hungry for love? Find food for that child. Is a rain forest hungry for preservation? Find food. Are there people on the streets, are they hungry for a home? Find food. Are nations at war, do they hunger for peace? Find food. Is anyone beaten down, is anyone cast aside, is anyone desperate from trying again and again and never being recognized; is anyone silenced, is anyone hungry for justice? Find food. When I become food, I become myself.

When the People were lost,
she found a Way.

The Way is infinite. It contains us all. The Way is not an ideology, it is not politics, it is not religion. It does not exclude variety. It is never doctrinaire. There is no arrogance in the Way. No pride. It does not force. Those who find the Way may not be correct, but they are good; they may not speak a proper language, but they live the truth; they may not take up banners and demonstrate for a cause, but they act with compassion. I search as deeply as I can. It is the finding, itself, that delivers me from being lost. The Way is written on my heart; it is inscribed upon my bones. Its pathways wind through my brain. Its wonders are the visions of my mind. Its destination is a beacon for my soul.

When the People became sick from a mysterious disease,
She went to the forest and found an herb
That healed them.

I cannot heal myself alone. My disease is not mine alone. I participate. I manifest in my body and my mind the wasting of the earth, the devastation of rain forests, the extinction of species, the pollution of our waters, the spoiling of our air. This message is sent out in languages as diverse as hummingbirds and whales. I have not heard deeply enough. I continue to be sick. Healing requires that I love all creatures and love the earth that is my home and my larger body. Healing will be work. I need to search with all who search. It will take every one of us to achieve the balance of healing. Together we need to bring the soil back to life. We need find an antidote for the poison. I need to do what can be done, make a compost heap, plant a tree.

When the People felt lonely or frightened,
When the People cried because their loved ones died,
When the People worried
And when their hearts felt like rocks in their chests,
Shell found stories to soothe their pain.

Stories connect me to a larger pattern, to the meaning of my life. I listen to the stories people tell, the stories my aged mother, and before her, my grandmother, told about their lives. The same story over and over, as though telling it for the first time, as though I have not heard this one a thousand times—so often I can tell it myself, word for word. What wisdom is there to alleviate the pain? The wisdom of the story, the mothers' stories, mine. I want to pass my story on, give not a solution but courage, acceptance, love to those who listen. I came through, the story says. I live. My life fits into some larger whole.

After many years,
The People gave Shell a new name
To tell her who she had become in their midst.
They called her "Finding Woman."

Eventually, I become what I do. Eventually, my identity is a perfect reflection of my activity. My acting and my being are the same. I am not the job I take on to support myself and my family. I have a friend who works with computers, but that is not how I identify her. She is the one who visits the nursing home every Tuesday. She starts a song; the old ones sing with her. Even those who cannot talk anymore, they hum along off key. She says she dreams of symphonies, impossible music soars in her sleep. She says she has no instrument to produce it in her waking life. That is not true. She has the old ones. They are the music. In their midst she has become the Singing One. I wonder who I have become.

All this time
The smooth round stone lay in the leather pouch
Over Finding Woman's heart.

Life is continual transformation. But something always remains, something fundamental, something that endures through the changing: a thread, a tone, a presence. In this presence I am. I am still, as things I thought essential pass away. I learn that people can die, all can be taken, my heart can break and be poured out. A bird sings while I wait for word, and then my loved one is dead. I can be alone and in the deepest grief and seem to have no one. My stomach aches with grief. I weep and, suddenly, inexplicably, I feel the breath of God. I feel drawn like a seed on the breath of God into the warm motherly heart of the Divine. I am held in the heart of God. So tender. So full. So knowing of all I thought was lost. In that heart everything is found. And I know with absolute certainty that I will never be alone.

In the cold
she could feel the stone's warmth.

Cold can kill. The deepest circles of Dante's hell are ice. Cold cuts my circulation; I conserve my blood to my heart. I try to remain alive. What happens bodily happens also in my spirit. I suffer from the cold. The cold of rejection. The cold of indifference. The cold of ridicule. I need to carry warm stones.

When she felt confused,
She listened for the stone's voice.

Confusion is many voices talking at once. All of them part of me. The voice of the mother argues with the voice of the child; the voice of the friend argues with the voice of the solitary; mind argues with heart; artist with philosopher; hermit with adventurer. It is a din. It is pandemonium—all the demons. Demons are angels cast aside. Angels unrecognized. They cry out to be heard. Their voices fuse—confusion.

I listen more deeply. In the center of the confusion is a voice that does not fuse but integrates. There is a voice that recognizes all the angels' voices. I sit still. I breathe. The din becomes a whisper like leaves scattering in the wind. I wait for the silence. Breathe. Wait. Listen. Each voice has its wisdom.

As she lived,
she learned Finding Stone's wisdom.

I do not want merely to live; I want to engage life. I want to squeeze life like a tree-ripened orange, to carry life like a child. I want life to be my lover. I want to breathe deeply and fill my lungs with life; let its blood rush to my head and out to my fingertips. I want to spread life around, plant it like seed, give it away as if it had no end, no limit, as if I were rich with it. I want to take life on like a warrior, to shake it, to wrestle, to tear it open to expose its heart. I want to weep with life, to tend its wounds, to rub pure oil down deep into life's pain and sing while life heals. I want to be swept up in life's adventure, to go where life calls me, to climb mountains, explore caves. I want to refuse life nothing.

As she wondered how to grow
From being a girl into being a woman,
She heard the Finding Stone whisper,
"Flow."

Sometimes I get in the way. I try to take hold, control the changes, manage the growth. But a flower does not control its growth; neither does a child. The time of transformation is not a time for choice but for awareness and developing understanding. I flow. I feel the currents of the self, all of them. I feel the mild flow and the tumult. I feel the currents join, inter-flow. I take time. I sit cross-legged under a tree and watch the river. I lie on the grass and gaze at the clouds. I listen to music. I listen to the rain, watch it collect in rivulets and flow. I stand in the rain with my face lifted. I experience change fully.

As she wondered how to give
The gift that was herself
To the People she loved,
She heard the Finding Stone whisper,
"Shine."

What do I have to give? In the moment I can know. The touch of a hand, a smile at a stranger on the street. What does the moment ask? Be present. Let the ground on which I stand be the basis for giving. See. Let love flow. That is what love does. Someone asks for alms; I know what my money is for. A lonely neighbor calls; I visit. A bird sings; I am still. Each moment is a request; I offer what I am. The gift that shines with the energy of love is received.

As she wondered how people learned to trust one another,
She heard the Finding Stone whisper,
"Receive."

I trust myself to know what is good for me. I honor myself. I keep myself from harm. Saying no to harm is a way of loving. I trust that which is worthy of trust, both in myself and in others. It is the only thing that is real in us. Trusting can be a difficult skill to develop, especially if I have learned early not to trust, if I believed it when the one who hurt me said, "Trust me, this is good for you." Receiving is the way to re-learn. Receiving does not mean to take anything anybody gives out. Receiving means keeping open, feeling what I feel, respecting my instincts, not denying what is in front of me. If someone tells me one thing and her eyes say something else, I request the truth. When I trust what I receive within myself, I become worthy of other people's trust. Soon a community of trust develops.

As she wondered how to pass her wisdom on
To the children born from her body and her soul,
She heard the Finding Stone whisper,
"Change."

Wisdom is change. Wisdom is both the process and the result of transformation. Wisdom creates, is in constant movement, bringing design to the universe. Wisdom dances; She plays alongside of God from the beginning; She is forever the child; She is the oldest one, who existed before all things, the ever-unfolding being of God. Wisdom is the essence of living. Maybe it cannot be passed on through lectures and books. I need to live, distill wisdom from experience. Wisdom is my commitment to life, my willingness to continue changing, developing, transforming. When I live my life and love the living, all of it—the births and the deaths, the fullness and the loss—I wring wisdom out of it. My life is distilled, and wisdom runs rich and strong, a fine essence, through every word and act.

As she wondered how to help her own children
Find their way along the confusing paths of the world,
She heard her Finding Stone whisper,
"Wait."

I wait. My children have their own way. I wait. They hear a call out of a future I can never know. They follow, despite the darkness, the unknowing, the pain. So I must let this generation be who they are and will become. My child, grown up, tells me what his life means. My child explains, sitting by the fireplace when he is twenty-three, that when he was nineteen he thought his life was ending, useless, that he had failed, that he did drugs, that he hit the streets. But he learned, he explains, how to survive. He learned that hard times would not destroy him. He learned how to come through. He is thankful for the freedom to find his way. I listen and remember the paths that opened for me. I remember the pulse of adventure, the draw of the unknown, the surprise of discovery, the intoxication of choice, the intensity of commitment. Even the mistakes were teachers.

As she lost people whom she loved
Because they traveled to the prairie
Or the mountain or the desert or another sea,
Or because they made the final journey to the stars,
She felt empty in her heart,
But she heard her Finding Stone whisper,
"Endure."

Loss stretches my soul. Loss widens my heart and leaves me standing on tiptoe at the road's end, watching. I stand in the road, but my yearning reaches to the Arizona desert, the wooded slopes of Vermont, the Dakota prairies, the Minnesota lakes; to a cabin at the tree line in the Rockies, the white sands of Florida beaches, a forest in Germany, a valley in the rain forest of Maui, the sheer cliffs of Kerry. From my heart, paths forged by those I love stretch around the world. They took what I gave them of myself and walked to the ends of the world and beyond, to the stars. The spaciousness of my heart is as large as anything I have lost, my home as extensive as all the places my loved ones have gone. I am large as life. I will endure.

As she grew old and was alone,
She heard her Finding Stone whisper,
"Continue."

I find reservoirs of courage in unlikely places. I know old people who live in broken-down houses with mud yards and loose stair railings. They live in dingy rooms over old cafes or hardware stores. They live behind the regular houses, on the alley, in sheds. One lives with fifty cats, wild, that crouch on cupboards, atop the fridge, under a broken-down sofa piled with rags. These people tell me miracles. They sing hymns. They search their souls. They dream. They memorize the world and tell stories if anyone will listen. One man's white hair springs around his face like Einstein's. A woman wears a feather boa and bright red lipstick, and she walks the street laughing about her boyfriends. A blind man still finds his way to the bus. In a shabby but spotless room, an old woman spreads out her albums, pointing at the fading images in sepia-colored photos, imprinting on my heart the names of those she has loved and lost. These are the old ones who continue. From them I receive the courage to live until I die.

As the young came to her for wisdom,
She heard her Finding Stone whisper,
"Remember."

"Hold all of life together," my soul's voice speaks. "Remember the connections between people, between species, between time and space. Remember the passage from age to age, the cycles of the seasons, the way your legs felt when you were a child, running. Remember the intercourse of nations, the wars, the way they ended, the aftermath, the struggles, the recurrence, the futility of it all, the non-resolutions; the faces of the people in *Life Magazine* a long time ago, in the newsreels, then on television right while it happened, the horror. Remember how your knees felt, kneeling. Remember the sweet smell of roses, the wood-moss smell of soil. Remember those who died, the feel of your own mother, fragile, her bones delicate like relics of sparrows, while you held her and sang lullabies. Remember how the heart is made of thinnest glass and shatters. Remember how the heart is made of petals and blooms. Remember while you take the young ones in your arms and tell them stories."

And as her body became like a winter leaf
Blown across the snow,
She heard her Finding Stone whisper,
"Come Home."

There is a time to die. Our culture fears death, tries to keep the body alive at all costs, sees death as failure. But death is homing. Death, when life is full and the body is a winter leaf, opens the pathway home. My soul longs for home. Heaven. The Heart of God. Oneness with the universe. Union with Ultimate Being. Breakthrough. Transcendence of limits imposed by matter. Freedom of spirit. Union of spirits. Communion. Vision. Beatific vision.

Finding Woman went down to the white beach
By the cold blue sea.

At the end of anything, I return to the beginning. I trace a circle. I
bring it to a close. I allow myself to see, to understand, to feel the truth
that everything in life—all that makes me who I am, all my gifts,
everything I give to others; all the content of my struggles; all the
strength I pull up from my soul, from the marrow of my bones—all
of it has been present from the beginning. Everything in life is folded
into that first sense of self and my place in the continuum of creation.
I unfold. I live it out. And I return.

She lifted her medicine pouch from around her neck
And removed the Finding Stone.

All that life gives must be given back. All I hold must be returned. Whatever makes me who I am—that quality of uniqueness, that spark, that turn of phrase, that way of looking straight out and clear, that tenderness of touch, that intensity of will, that whirlwind in the brain twisting opposites together and creating the unexpected, the love that penetrates and receives, the stories told, the songs sung, the laughter like no one else's laughter, my tears over hummingbirds with broken wings, my passion to keep the trees tall and strong and unmolested, my nights alone by the fire under the stars, my nights with loved ones when the wind battered the house and the snow swirled, my days walking to work and to the market, my swimming in the river with the children, my crying out to the mountains echoing a cacophony of the sound the world makes—I must give it back. All of it back. Back to the beginning. Give it up. I let it go. I let it be. It will be part of everything I became during all this life and will continue when I go beyond.

She placed it on the beach,
And it caught the light of the setting sun
As it lingered at the edge
Between the grey-blue water and the sky.

I set down everything I love. I stand looking out over the ocean. A gull dips into a wave, rises and floats on the wind. All those who went before me gather on the horizon. They sing to me: "Go lightly into each new life; that is the wisdom of death. Give. Let the gift catch light. Let life, your life, your self, be light. Engage in alchemy. Stand on the beach at the edge of the world and turn your gifts into light. Let the Finding Stone transform you. Let your wisdom be transformed. Let your hopes, your dreams, your entire life be transformed. Set it down upon the beach. Let the sun fill it. It will become the sun. It will shine. It will linger on the edge between earth and sky. Light. You will be light. And death will not be able to hold you."

She listened to the whispered language of land and sea,
Talking.

I come at last to an understanding. An understanding of the language of the earth, of life itself. The language of my bones, the language of my children being born, the language of my flesh being stretched, the language of love. The language of trees talking with the wind, of snakes tracking the sand, of whales singing love songs, of stars exploding, of volcanoes spewing melted rock to recreate the earth, of icebergs slipping off glaciers, thundering into the sea. The language of the blood coursing through my body, and the bodies of bears, of the salmon, of everything wild and tame, of the bird and the squirrel who took for food the bird's blue egg. The language of the world, a wondrous song, a symphony. A hymn and a cry. Yearning and satisfaction. Crazed pain and glory. The language of creation talking with God. It is my prayer.

She felt she was complete.

What more is there? This is peace, the smile when everything is done and I sit in my rocking chair, my mind empty of thought, aware only of soft breeze from the porch and the wash of light through burnished yellow leaves. This is breath, slow, easy, in and out, and no hurry because there is no where to go, because it is done. This is the sweetness of closing my eyes, the drift of oncoming sleep, the beginning of dreams. This is the procession of faces, of ghosts, the spirits of all I have loved, passing through my mind and heart, present as they have always been present, never lost. I have never been alone. This is welcome recognition. I am complete. I am whole. I am good, and I am the one I am.

Finding Woman looked for a long time
At the smooth round stone
Lying on the sand,
Catching the last light of the setting sun.

Love. Love is the final lesson. Love is the first and last impulse that creates me. I put down what is most precious, most loved. I look at it for a long time. I stand watching the horizon where a child disappeared just moments ago as she traveled on to find her own life. I stand gazing at my loved one's face, chiseled with death, beautiful as a Michelangelo. I look long at my own life. Only now is it possible to put it down, when all of it is loved. All the joys; I see how they have made me strong. All the accomplishments; I see how I have built on the wisdom of others, how we are connected, part of a creation that continues. All the pain, the struggle, the loss; I feel the tenderness, the compassion that remains. All the failures, the mistakes; I see how I have learned. All the yearning, all the prayers, all the reaching out; I see that I am large, that I am round, that I breathe with the world. I look long at all that I lay down. I look with love.

"Someone will find you," she said.

The cycle continues. Nothing of life is lost. Everything each person makes of life goes on. It spreads out. It is there to be picked up. Things I never knew I made, words I forgot I said, someone finds them. Someone picks them up and wears them though life in a medicine pouch, in the mind, in the heart. At last I know who I am, and still I do not know. I go on in ways I never dreamed. My most insignificant act could be a Finding Stone for someone else who picks it up and carries it through life. From that fragment of my soul, someone I never knew—or someone as treasured as my own child—may distill wisdom and love. Nothing is ever lost.

"Never Ends,"
The Finding Stone whispered back
into her soul.

"Never Ends"—this is the promise. It is the promise the land gives. It is the promise of the sea and of the unending sky beyond the farthest star. This is the promise of God. "Never Ends" has always been the promise. From the beginning.

Christin Lore Weber is an experienced author, religious educator, spiritual guide, and lecturer. Her quiet quest for truth and the meaning of life began early, when she was a child growing up on Lake of the Woods in Minnesota, at the border of the United States with Canada. Of herself she says, "I've spent my life finding stones. I roll stones around in my hand. I know them in mind and heart. Stones of life. I am all that I have ever been: a nun, a beloved, a wife, a mother, a soul guide; one who makes ritual, who makes stories, who makes poems, who makes bread and salad and delicious cookies. I am a child and a student of life."

Her love for spirituality led her to a fourteen-year commitment as a Sister of St. Joseph, during which time she pursued knowledge in the humanities and theology. She earned a B.A. degree in literature and drama from Viterbo College, LaCrosse, Wisconsin; an M.A. degree in theology from St. John's University, Collegeville, Minnesota; and a doctor of ministry degree from United Theological Seminary, New Brighton, Minnesota.

After a twenty year career in educational, parish, and human service institutions, Christin's writing career began in 1983 with the publication of her first book, *Caring Community*. Her subsequent books include *WomanChrist: A New Vision of Feminist Spirituality*, *Blessings: A WomanChrist Reflection on the Beatitudes*, and *Circle of Mysteries: The Women's Rosary Book*.

Christin and her husband, John, make their home on the West Coast.

If you enjoyed FINDING STONE,
you'll value these other LuraMedia books:

CIRCLE OF STONES
Woman's Journey To Herself
by Judith Duerk

OVER 150,000 COPIES SOLD!

A guide for women searching for their inner wisdom. A personal yet universal journey to the essence of the feminine. Used in women's groups, retreats, and workshops all over the country. $11.95.

I SIT LISTENING TO THE WIND
Woman's Encounter Within Herself
by Judith Duerk

The second book in the CIRCLE OF STONES SERIES. Explores the inner masculine. A guide for women everywhere who are searching for their true selves in a world of changing values and roles. $11.95.

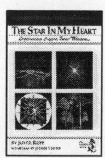

THE STAR IN MY HEART
Experiencing Sophia, Inner Wisdom
by Joyce Rupp

Opening the path to the inward journey, Rupp brings a deep awareness of Sophia, the spirit of inner wisdom. Ideal for personal meditation or as a resource/study book for groups. $11.95.

LuraMedia books are available in bookstores,
or call 1-800-FOR-LURA to order.
Ask for our free catalog!

LURAMEDIA™